Difficult Differences

Carlos Piera

Difficult Differences
Diferencias Difíciles

Selected, translated from the Spanish, and introduced by
Roberta Ann Quance

Shearsman Books

This edition first published in the United Kingdom in 2025 by
Shearsman Books
P.O. Box 4239
Swindon
SN3 9FN

Shearsman Books Ltd Registered Office
30–31 St. James Place, Mangotsfield, Bristol BS16 9JB
(this address not for correspondence)

EU AUTHORISED REPRESENTATIVE:
Lightning Source France, 1 Av. Johannes Gutenberg, 78310 Maurepas, France
Email: compliance@lightningsource.fr

www.shearsman.com

ISBN 978-1-84861-920-3

Original poems copyright © Carlos Piera, 1972, 1985, 1990, 2005, 2013, 2025.
Translation, introduction and notes copyright © Roberta Quance, 2025

The right of Carlos Piera to be identified as the author and of Roberta Quance
to be identified as the translator of this work has been asserted by them in
accordance with the Copyrights, Designs and Patents Act of 1988.
All rights reserved.

Diferencias Difíciles was originally published in 2025
by Libros de la Resistencia, Madrid, and we are grateful
for their permission to publish this edition.

CONTENTS

Introduction   8

De *Versos* / from *Verses* (1972)

16	Till the Future Dares / Till the Future Dares	17
18	*Aquí también hubo elementos simples…* / Here, too, there were simple elements…	19
20	De nuestros movimientos naturales / On Our Natural Movements	21
22	*Los caballos de casco despótico y libre…* / The horses' free and despotic hooves…	23
24	Nabí / Nabi	25
26	Ítaca de abajo / Lower Ithaca	27
28	*Por la ametralladora, el cuchillo y la muñeca…* / On my tommy-gun, knife, and doll…	29
30	Dos versos que llaman "para poder" / Two Poems Called "In Order to"	31
32	Palabras entre el hereje y el diablo / Words Between the Heretic and the Devil	33

De *Antología para un papagayo* / from *Anthology for a Parrot* (1985)

34	*La nostalgia del bien, del mal…* / Nostalgia for the good. As for the bad…	35
36	Gusto en verlos / Pleased to see them	37
38	Banda / The Gang	39
40	Línea del Pacífico / Pacific Coastline	41
42	Poema sobre el paro / Out of Work Poem	43
44	Ninfa / Nymph	45
46	Puntos de vista sobre las sirenas / Points of View on Mermaids	47
50	Ermitaño / Hermit	51
52	Casandra / Cassandra	53
54	Pastor llega, descubre el mar / A Shepherd Arrives, Discovers the Sea	55
56	Rambla / Rambla	57

De *De lo que viene como si se fuera* /
from *On what is coming as if it were going* (1990)

58	Upstate / Upstate	59
60	La mala hierba / The Tough Old Weed	61
62	Retrato / Portrait	63
64	Quebrado / Fractioned	65
66	Alacrán / Scorpion	67
68	Del movimiento del camaleón / On the Movement of the Chameleon	69
70	Erizo / Hedgehog	71
72	Legado / Legacy	73
74	Alfilador / Knifegrinder	75
76	Gato muerto / Dead Tomcat	77
78	Letanía del Día de Difuntos / Litany for the Day of the Dead	79
84	La muerte que mendiga para comprar droga / Death Begging Money for a Fix	85
86	Revenant / Revenant	87
88	Primero de Mayo / May 1st	89
90	Ahasuerus / Ahasuerus	91
92	Breve ensayo sobre la poesía / Brief Essay on Poetry	93

De *Religio y otros poemas* / from *Religio and other poems* (2005)

94	Religio. Seis misterios / Religio. Six Mysteries	95
120	Espectro brevemente / A Specter, Briefly	121
124	Vox clamantis / Vox clamantis	125
126	Victimae paschali laudes / Victimae paschali laudes	127
128	Encuentro una rata muerta en un jardín japones / I Come Across a Dead Rat in a Japanese Garden	129

Otros poemas de *Apartamentos de alquiler. Obra reunida* /
Other poems from *Apartments for Rent. Collected Work* (2013)

130	C.P. Responde a ciertas objeciones / C.P. Replies to Certain Objections	132
132	El tiempo perdido / Time lost	133
134	Pueden caer historias porque hay lluvias constantes… / In the constant rain stories…	135

136	*El mar, que sólo sabe a sal, y el aire…* /	
	The sea that only smacks of salt…	137
138	A una ausente / To Someone Who Is Not Here	139
140	Sentadito en su tejado / Sitting Up on His Roof	141
142	Nana de Gaza / Gaza Lullaby	143
144	Cuento de Navidad y tal /	
	A Christmas Tale, That Sort of Thing	145

        Notes   146

A Bird's Eye View of *Difficult Differences*

Roberta Ann Quance

The idea for this anthology dates back to early 2021. I had finished a translation of 'Religio', a poem it was a priority for me to make better known – as if in defiance of the circumscribed world the pandemic had imposed – and when my version was accepted for a New York journal (*Circumference*, no. 9, 2021) I began to think about how a broader selection of the poetry Carlos Piera had written over the years might look. I remembered other translations, some very early ones, that I had done at the request of a Madrid publisher and friend and which, to my astonishment, had held up very well.[1]

On that particular occasion I had published translations of five poems for an anthology that came out in the Edwin Mellen Press, an academic publisher, nearly thirty years ago. Although the book did not attract much attention, neither good nor bad (and unjustly so), I recall that the author and I had regarded the translations as a minor miracle. "It's just that you sound very good in English". "That's all your doing". And so on. Each attributed any successes to the other party, as often happens in Spanish culture.

But if Carlos were not who he is – a theorist of meter and master of an English that has often allowed him to pass for a native speaker – I would not have dared to take the translation of his work up again.[2] To me, the good result we achieved in 1997 – and later – came down to personal affinity and our life in common. Maybe also to the fact that Carlos acknowledged his debt to authors in English who had meant a lot to me (Eliot, Yeats, Auden…). We complement one another, I thought. In time –and with a certain amount of experience to my credit – I grew certain that to translate was not simply a linguistic matter but rather an exercise in reading and interpretation, in which the translator, from within his or

---

[1] *A Bilingual Anthology of Spanish Poetry: The Generation of 1970: v. 43 (Hispanic Literature)*, ed. Luis Ramos-García (Lewiston, NY: Edwin Mellen Press, 1998).

[2] For some appreciation of Carlos's linguistic work see Esther Torrego, ed., *Of Grammar, Words, and Verses: In honor of Carlos Piera* (Amsterdam: John Benjamins, 2012).

her own language and person, assumed the poem as their own. There was, I thought, an invitation to translate implicit in Carlos's wish for readers to use and dwell inside a poem temporarily as if it were an "apartamento de alquiler" (apartment for rent).[3]

In the nineties, I thought a great deal about the question of voice in poetry and if I had managed to find an appropriate diction, a register and tone that was right, in order to convey the irony and the desperation that could often be heard in Carlos's work, as well as its melancholy.

From his very first book (*Versos,* 1972) Carlos had gone against the grain of what was officially successful in Spain (*Nueve novísimos poetas españoles*), writing verse that did not entirely fit into the group album of the seventies which that anthology was meant to be. While scholars in Spain and abroad hurried to promote and publicize a new "culturalist" mode of writing, a post-68 mode, purged of social concern in the Sartrean sense, Carlos turned to poetry to register his philosophical doubts about late Francoist culture and the future to which his country was headed.

He had been officially "disciplined" (and finally expelled) by the Universidad Complutense of Madrid for anti-Franco protest and forced to complete his degree in Romance philology at the Universitat de Barcelona. Once back in Madrid and after a stint working at Salvat publishers, he teamed up with like-minded friends to found the *Equipo Comunicación,* which took a special interest in the "linguistic turn" in European thought.[4] His interest in linguistics and in generative grammar led to the receipt of a fellowship to study in the United States. And so he came to be associated with UCLA, MIT, and Cornell, either as a student, visiting scholar, or professor. (And Cornell, at the beginning of the fall term 1980, is where we met.)

Most of the poems from *Antología para un papagayo* (1985) date from that long period abroad (1974–1983) and reflect obliquely on the writer's condition as an outsider (there, for example, is 'Pleased to see them' or the

---

[3] On the question of the reader of a poem as a "user" see Rafael Sánchez Ferlosio, *Las semanas del jardín. Semana segunda* (Madrid: Nostromo, 1974), and the argument that this is a radical way of distinguishing lyric poetry from narrative. One does not "say" a narrative as if it were an enunciation, even if it is autobiographical or even if it is oral.

[4] A recent exhibition at the Universidad Autónoma de Madrid, *Equipo Comunicación. Anti-franquismo, edición y debate* (1968–1979) from 28/10/2024 to 6/12/2024, curated by Rosa Benéitez. Juan Albarrán Diego and Paula Barreiro López, looked at the project in its different facets.

allegorical 'Hermit'). Carlos lived this part of his life as a kind of interim, a near-exile that could hardly resolve his sense of family or civic duty, even as he adapted to a congenial professional life. When he returned to Spain in 1983 it was in the hope of taking part in the changes heralded by the Transition to democracy. But the years of the *Movida*, as eventually became clear, brought a demobilization of the left and the beginning of a slow erosion of the status of the intellectual. A society was forming in which he did not feel he fit very well. And so a fault-line deepened in his verse, visible as an oscillation between hope and disillusionment.[5]

Linguistically, there is a clear propensity for contradiction, as the title *De lo que viene como si se fuera* (1990) signals, as the need for self-defense comes to the fore (with an incipient bestiary of hedgehog, scorpion, or chameleon). How can one make a home for oneself in a country that was in some respects moving in the opposite direction he desired? Spain had veered to the right, following the US and the UK's neoliberalism, and some intellectuals concluded it was time to salvage what one could. That was the implicit aim behind one of the most significant Spanish journals of the time, *La Balsa de la Medusa* (1987–2011), of which Carlos was a founding member and, when his turn came, a director.

They were not auspicious years. For a time the poet grows quiet, devoting intellectual effort to essays and editorial work.

When he publishes again it is to bring out a work that suggests a longed-for inner renewal.[6] And 'Religio' (2005), a unique work in Spanish, in the line of mystical poetry, comes close to being a celebration. From the mid-nineties onward Carlos had been studying the work of the different masters of Buddhism. Although he speaks ironically of his lack of discipline and inconsistency, he acquired a considerable personal library on the sacred texts and on the different schools and exegesis they offered. However, his interest was not primarily theoretical: he read and meditated. And he

---

[5] Credit is due the late Mari Pepa Palomero (*Poetas de los 70. Antología de poesía española contemporánea* (Madrid: Hiperión, 1987) for pointing out Carlos's penchant for contradiction (see p. 217). The *Movida* refers to a short explosion of creativity in the arts in the wake of Franco's death in 1975 and is captured best by Pedro Almodóvar's early films.

[6] In unpublished notes from the late 90s he writes: "'Despertar de la Historia': eso quería el Stephen Dedalus de Joyce. A mí algo comparable a la Historia me atormentaba y yo no lo sabía. Le he dado un nombre a eso que me atormentaba: el de Samsara, ni mejor ni peor que cualquier otro, pero el único significativo que me ha surgido". *Samsara* is a Sanskrit term for noise and hell and frenzy, among other things.

made this commitment compatible with his teaching at the Universidad Autónoma of Madrid and his work as an essayist and editor.

Over the years, as the spectacle of an end to world peace loomed (the Gulf War in 1990–91 cast a long shadow), I heard him talk about what he had discovered in Eastern wisdom. I did not share his practice, which is to say, I did not meditate in any regular fashion. But I thought I grasped the experience from which his verse arose or at least how that sort of experience could be captured in poetry. To translate 'Religio' I recalled John of the Cross and the late poetry of T.S. Eliot, authors I had studied in some depth at different moments in life.

In the Latin roots of the word *religion* there is a core concept, the re-tying or re-binding of (our understanding of) all things in the universe. If the etymology has anything to do with Carlos's title, it may be simply to advise the reader that the poem arises from out of an experience of this unity. Each of the six "mysteries" into which the long poem is divided is vocative: the lyric voice addresses something named "Lu", as if addressing a principle that gives order and meaning to the world. "Lu" is introduced in the first line of the long poem as a "sílaba simiente" [seed-syllable], a concept in Buddhism, which the poem eventually makes clear is a kind of whole or desideratum invoked by the poet as if it were a loved one. *Lu* is a syllable that calls forth many different words in Spanish (and some in English as well): *luz* [light], *luminoso* [luminous], *luna* [moon], *lúcido* [lucid], *iluminar* (illuminate), *dilucidar* [elucidate]… and therefore it is not translated as such but allowed to remain as a "seed" sign common to both Spanish and English.

I saw for myself, once again, that the resources of language on which mysticism drew – East or West – had a ground in common: writers employed the language of paradox or of the "negative way", a sometimes hesitating speech in order to bring the listener closer to an experience that, by definition, falls outside language proper.[7] And this problem of expression may lead a reader to think that the referent is only language itself, as one critic has ventured.[8]

I speak of the experience of a group of writers but Carlos would not presume to set himself beside them. His experience with meditation is not

---

[7] On this question see Kevin Hart, *The Trespass of the Sign* (Cambridge: Cambridge UP, 1989). Frits Staal (*Exploring Mysticism. A Methodological Essay,* Berkeley, University of California Press, 1975), has suggested that the mystical experience may derive from a pre-linguistic state.

[8] Ángel Luján, "La vida sagrada", *Revista de Libros* [Madrid] (February 2006), p. 2.

about an intimation of God; Buddhism is a-theistic. Characteristically, too, he downplays his "competence" in the matter, remembering that for someone travelling between Madrid, Amsterdam, and Boston, as he did, and learning from different teachers, he was undisciplined. But Buddhism is there in the background. Taking its point of departure in Tao (the Way), it teaches harmony of the self with nature and becoming. Poetically we are dealing with a philosophy that permeates the haiku tradition and the work of masters like Basho. But, as the Chinese poet Han Shan explains, in Gary Snyder's wonderful translation of a ninth-century classic, you find your own way: "Men ask the way to Cold Mountain/ Cold Mountain: there's no through trail".[9]

'Religio', however, is such a consummate poem that it is tempting to read it as a watershed in Carlos's poetry, marking a before and after. And that is because it is by definition about a moment of plenitude. One that is only glimpsed but that for that very reason does not lock into a narrative. It has no beginning or end. And so, when it came time to edit it within a collection of his poetry, 'Religio' posed the question of how its reading would affect what came before or what follows. Observing that the long poem was placed at the beginning of Carlos's collected work (in reverse order of composition), Miguel Casado has remarked that it seems like an "illumination" that lightens darker poems of ordinary days.[10]

In this selection 'Religio' takes its place in a chronological order but without becoming a piece set into a narration. Although the poetry coming before or after it can, of course, be read in its light, nothing is built or erected upon it, The experience captured can, however, be read as issuing from a stubborn disenchantment with Western pretensions. Who is the Messiah? What role falls to the prophet or the intellectual (as the poet asks very early on in 'Nabi')? Steeped in the Bible and especially the Old Testament, Carlos has signed his name to poems that can be read as questioning authority, not with the aim of casting doubt on the search for what is just but to urge humility and prudence on the part of those who undertake that search.

---

[9] For the complete text see *Anthology of Chinese Literature*, ed. by Cyril Burch (New York: Random Hose-Evergreen, 1965), pp. 194-202. On the influence of Buddhism (in American poetry) see the volume *Beneath a Single Moon. Buddhism in Contemporary American Poetry* (Boston: Shambhala, 1991).

[10] See 'El huésped del Monte Lu', in Miguel Casado, *La ciudad de los nómadas* (Madrid: Libros de la Resistencia, 2018), pp. 111-15.

Can the poet speak for others while at the same time expressing the conviction that he is "nobody" (like Ulysses)? Or feeling his own disauthorization? In modern times who has ever asked the poet to speak? Carlos imagines himself as *other* in order to talk about his own circumstances but that is often, ironically, as an *other* who does not have a voice himself. And so there is Ahasuerus, the Wandering Jew, who regrets having spoken, or the Palestinian mother, who sings a lullaby before a bomb may fall. The worst fate is to have no voice or to have one that is scorned: to be a Cassandra or an "old weed", unable to do much more than scream. Out of such contradictions poetry emerges.

A practical note on which to conclude: I have been asked how these translations were done. Poet and translator hit on a simple but effective way to work and one which is respectful of different roles. When as a translator I had a draft of the collection ready (which I felt capable of answering for), I asked Carlos to read through it, and then we sat down together, with everything on the table, translations and originals, to see what did and didn't work. In the discussion that followed and in the reading aloud, we considered what changes were in order and – even if not many – what cuts would be made. We wanted to produce texts that sounded true to their origins. And, to my ears, would have something of the emotional charge in the second language that was there in the first.[11] Needless to say, the responsibility for errors in judgment on that point is my own.

At the end of the book are notes meant to clarify cultural allusions for a foreign reader or younger Spanish generations.

The title *Difficult Differences* did not, however, come from the translation experience. It comes from a line in 'Points of view on mermaids' and attests to the challenge of translating the inhuman to the human. And so the title is conceived as a homage to the difficulty the poet faces: to write from the philosophical difference between nature – together with its raw pain – and the possibilities for articulation of that difference which language affords.

---

[11] It was helpful to me (though sobering) to be reminded that lyric poetry derives its force from resources in the mother tongue that are personal and give a specific timbre to "voice", as Mutlu Konuk Blasing argues in *Lyric Poetry* (Princeton, NJ: Princeton University Press, 2007).

Diferencias Difíciles

Difficult Differences

De *Versos* (1972)

TILL THE FUTURE DARES

Demasiado supieron ser sublimes en piedra.
Naturaleza y gente nos los han conservado
casualmente,
restos de presente pensado pasado. Todavía somos la posteridad.
Porque no podemos
hacer monumentos son ellos valientes y porque seremos
no piedra o virtudes, sino unos recuerdos banales y amargos como
                                                                                   [unas infancias,
como unas canciones de hace un año, cuando
al alzar los ojos sabios en estatuas
ya no haya herederos.

From *Verse* (1972)

TILL THE FUTURE DARES

They knew too well how to be sublime in stone.
Nature and people have kept them for us
accidentally,
the remains of a present thought to be past.
We are still posterity.
Because we are not able
to build monuments, they are valiant; and because
we will not be stone or virtue but memories instead –
banal and bitter like some people's childhood
or last year's tunes – when we lift
our eyes in wisdom to statues
there shall be no successors.

> *fatti non foste a viver come bruti.*
> Dante, *Inferno*, XXVI, 119

Aquí también hubo elementos simples,
el agua y la tierra trabados en lucha y naufragios oscuros.
Luego fue retórica. A la larga morir es inútil
y todos los hombres acaban en literatura.
Aquí estaba Ulises fétido y cansado dando absurdas órdenes. Mar, que serás perfecto
porque los recuerdos no han mentido nunca, bendito es aquello
que tiene un solo nombre como el Mediterráneo
y los hombres que dieron los nombres y están en olvido.

> *fatti no foste a viver come bruti*
> Dante, *Inferno,* XXVI, 119

Here, too, there were simple elements,
water and earth locked in struggle and obscure founderings.
Later it was rhetoric. In the long run dying is useless
and all men wind up as literature.
Here stood Ulysses, stinking and weary, issuing absurd commands. Sea,
you who surely are perfect,
for memories have never told untruths, blessed be
that which has but one name, like the Mediterranean,
and the men who gave the names and who lie forgotten.

De nuestros movimientos naturales

Esta ciudad de tierras altas va
a ser igual de hermosa cuando se olvide y quede
pura pureza en nuestra muerte el aire
sin nombre de diciembre.
Si los sabios admiran
amor entre animales y aun sólo movimientos, cómo entender
esta naturaleza de mi especie, el saber hacer casas y entonces
no tener casa nunca, sino apenas saberes.

On Our Natural Movements

This upland city is going to be
every bit as beautiful when it's forgotten and
there remains, sheer purity upon our passing,
the nameless December air.
If wise men admire
love among animals and even only movements, what is one to make
of the nature of my species, the knowing how to build a house and
then never having a house, instead just the knowing?

Los CABALLOS de casco despótico y libre cruzan el polvo levantándolo
de infancias más estrechas y tristes que su recuerdo, entonces,
a la caída de la tarde, ya sin sol, en víspera de lunes.
Artificiales cuerpos geométricos regularmente siguen encerrando a los
                                                      [niños atónitos
nadie sabe por qué. ¡Qué extrañas clases, las de geografía!
De la muerte se ve solamente una mancha encarnada en el cine,
pero de los ríos nos dijeron menos: el nombre.

THE HORSES' FREE and despotic hooves kick up dust
across childhoods sadder and more cramped than recall
allows, when the sun goes down and evening faces Monday.
Man-made geometrical bodies regularly lock amazed
children away, who knows why. Such strange classes,
geography! Death was only a red stain on the cinema screen,
but of the rivers we were told even less: their name.

Nabí

O el intelectual: Fecit sibimet umbraculum ibi, et sedebat
subter illud in umbra, donec videret quid acciderit civitati.
                Jonás 4, 5

Mira sucediéndose el mar y las olas más cerca,
mira (y desconfía de la erosión) sus límites. Mira las ciudades costeras,
la contraposición más simple, el elemento, la anulación de antónimos,
                              [el orden.
De noche es cuando el cielo se mueve y hay leyes humanas en astros. Sujeto
a las cuerdas del sol, a los azules de aparente violencia, nombraste
cuál había de ser tu tierra, tu cuidado
donde vivir y en qué corrales ácidos tomar el pan y el agua con la calma
                              [del mediodía. Elegiste.
Ardía el día agosto por causas remotísimas.
Dejaste las leyes de noche, jamás vigilaste
veinticuatro horas. Luego, corrompiéndose en verdes y grises el pan y
                              [las aguas,
entre dos implacables planos paralelos alzaste
un sombrajo, Jonás, y esperabas.
Cómo pediste ayuda, sentado allí, sentado, y todo para
que ardiera una maldita ciudad como tu piel quemada, donde tanta
mutación en un solo oscurecimiento
confluía.

Nabí

Or The Intellectual: Fecit sibimet umbraculum ibi, et sedebat
subter illud in umbra, donce videret quid acciderit civitati.
                                                                    Jonah 4: 5

Look at the sea succeeding itself and the waves coming closer,
look (mistrusting erosion) at its limits. Look at the cities by the coast,
the simplest comparison, the element, its annulment of opposites, order.
It's night when the heavens are in motion and human law looks to the
                                                                    [orbs. Bound
to the ropes of the sun, to blues apparently violent,
you singled out
which was to be your land, the object of your concern,
where you would live and in what sour yards
you would have your bread and water in the calm of midday. You chose.
The withered day burned for reasons exceedingly remote.
You left off studying the laws at night, you never
watched twenty-four hours running. Later with the bread
and water decomposing into gray and green,
between two implacable parallel planes you set up
a sun-shade, Jonah, and you waited.
How you asked for help as you sat, and you sat, and all so
one damned city would go up in flames like your sunburnt flesh, where
                                                                    [so much
change in only one darkness
was merging.

Ítaca de abajo

Marchó, nadie le dijo adiós, y es asombroso
que al volver nada hubiera cambiado sino él.
Se compró un traje nuevo, trató de presumir. Fue descubierto.
En un jardín con polvo del verano sintió pasar las horas escondido.
Un niño le pidió dinero y no tenía.
Le llovió encima y no tenía abrigo.
Y pensó entonces: «En remotos tiempos,
hombres con cara de caballo y barba negra
en el desierto hicieron por vanidad, o por algún cansancio,
esta ciudad tan grande, luego hay cosas
que no son necesarias».

Lower Ithaca

He left, no one told him goodbye, and it's amazing
that on his return nothing had changed but him.
He bought himself a new suit, tried to show off. He was found out.
Hiding in a garden full of summer's dust, he felt the hours go by.
A child asked him for money and he had none.
It rained on him and he had no coat.
And then he thought: "In far-off times, in the desert,
men with black beards and horse-like faces,
out of vanity or some weariness of spirit, built
this city that seems so big, so there are things
that are not necessary."

> *La bataille est merveilluse e pesant.*
> *Canción de Roldán*, v. 3381

Por la ametralladora y el cuchillo y la muñeca
que fueron mis juguetes, enemigo, por estos
muertos despanzurrados,
antes de que me mates, yo te juro
que nunca tuve armas, ni juguetes, ni muertos,
ni siquiera enemigo, lo más indispensable.

> *La bataille est merveilluse e pesant.*
> *Chanson de Roland*, v. 3381

ON MY TOMMY GUN, knife and doll, all
of which were my toys and on these
dead men in disarray,
to you, dear enemy, I swear
before you kill me, I never
had any weapons, toys or dead men's bodies
or even an enemy, the most necessary thing of all.

Dos versos que se llaman «para poder»

I

Camaleón en fábrica de cemento

Como unos vientos, como tempestades,
en la más infinita fatiga, tirando,
como si fueran guerras y tú fueras
obstinado o leal, crees o quieres
forjar viajes o fabricar sucesos
para poder volver a donde siempre
banalmente estuviste y sentir algo
de existencia en tus venas de color de pared.

II

Azafato o simplemente ejecutivo

Los aviones, como son de plástico,
casi no pesan en las incesantes
visiones del viajero de avión habitual,
que permanentemente miente viajes
para poder hablar.

Two Poems Called "In Order to"

I

Chameleon in a Cement Factory

Like some winds, some storms,
in uttermost weariness, soldiering on
as if they were wars and you were
obstinate or loyal, you believe or you wish to
fabricate events and make up travels
in order to go back to where
you always were in the banal sense and feel
something of existence in your veins the color of wall.

II

An Air Steward, or Just an Executive

The airplanes, as they are made of plastic,
have almost no weight in the incessant
visions of the frequent flyer
who speaks of his travels all the while
in order to have something to say.

Palabras entre el hereje y el diablo

H. Escribo para ciegos. Me ha traído la calma de la tarde.
    Pero me sé callar y sé
    que las ventanas de los días más secretos
    dan al silencio. Practicad silencio.
    No me imitéis.

D. Palabras. Cuando alguna amenaza sin nombre te siga
    ¿te bastará el horror para nombrarla? ¿De qué te sirve ver?
    Es más banal tu miedo que tu voz estudiada de cantante.

Words Between the Heretic and the Devil

H. – I write for blind men. Evening calm brought me here.
     But I know how to keep quiet and I know
     that the windows of the most secret days
     give onto silence. Practice silence.
     Do not as I do.

D. – Words. When a nameless threat is out to get you,
     will horror be enough to name it? What good is it for you to see?
     Your fear is more banal than your conservatory voice.

De *Antología para un papagayo* (1985)

Ya florecen los árboles, Juan,
mala seré de guardar

LA NOSTALGIA del bien. Del mal,
que seguía guardado dentro.
Del bien, pues, que las cosas pasan. Del mal que seguimos,
un adiós que dura una vida,
contenido como un ratón.
Es poeta quien no perdona. Tener esperanzas
es un tenaz recuerdo como todos los mayos,
verde y gris, donde esperan
(según, previsto azar, quebrando
vacío y solo las cortezas
mayo mismo es su propia
desmemoriada conmemoración)
otras tristezas y otra vez canciones,
por solidaridad, por poco tiempo,
nuestra contribución.

From *Anthology for a parrot* (1985)

> *The trees are all in bloom, Juan,*
> *What can hold me back?*
> Traditional folksong

NOSTALGIA FOR WHAT was good. As for the bad,
it went on within.
But for the good, at least, since these things pass. What's bad is we go on,
a lifetime of saying goodbye,
circumspect as a mouse.
Poets do not pardon. Having hopes
is a memory tenacious as all
months of May gray and green,
where (by foretold chance, breaking
only in the bark, May
being its own forgetful commemoration),
out of solidarity and only for a time,
other songs and other sadnesses
are our contribution.

Gusto en verlos

Se me han ido empañando los cristales.

Depositado en una Arcadia, compro
felicidad de otros en sus tiendas.

En paz con los castaños y las lluvias
dejan el bosque y su cobijo a veces.
Se congregan al paso, se sonríen,
desaparecen como los tejones.

Yo, que no sé guardar para el invierno,
con mi indulgencia desde mis rendijas,
yo, el tipo de detrás de las ventanas,
quería ser normal.

Pleased to See Them

My glasses are fogging up.

Here in the middle of Arcadia, I buy
other people's happiness in their shops.

They leave their woods and shelters sometimes,
making peace with the chestnut trees and the rain.
They gather briefly, smile at one another,
and then disappear like badgers.

I, who do not know how to save for the winter,
look at them indulgently through the cracks,
I, the man from behind the window,
who wanted to be normal.

Banda

Nadie ha ganado esta batalla, pero los que la hemos perdido
¡odiamos ahora tanto la familiaridad!
Consentimos metidos en casas el trato de antes,
eludiéndonos unos a otros, sabiendo
que es volver a lo más atroz de la niñez.
Este tiempo que no hemos querido, un espacio entre noches,
ni deja solo ni acompaña. Entonces,
alcohol, jardinería, matemáticas
y estar serios, como los niños serios,
silenciosos y tensos, como cuando
gritaron: Al ataque.

The Gang

There were no winners in this battle, but how we hate
the familiarity now, we who lost! Keeping
to home, we allow them to treat us like before,
we avoid one another, knowing
this is to go back to the worst part of childhood.
A time no one asked for, a space between nights,
that won't leave you alone or keep you company.
So here's to alcohol, gardening and math,
and the deadpan face that sobersided
children get, quiet and tense, like the time
they shouted: Get ready! Charge!

Línea del Pacífico

No es costa ésta de la que partir
salvo para esos viajes de que vuelves distinto
o no vuelves. Allí
marinos borrachos en playas muy blancas y aquí
un continente inerte. De esta putrefacción
discreta de tortuga sin tener dónde ir
y esta animal, descomunal cordura,
constantes las orillas, la marea, el océano
(será adorado el sol), sólo quedarán islas.

Pacific Coastline

This is not a coast from which to depart –
save for those voyages from which you come back changed
or not at all. Over there are
inebriate sailors on very white beaches and here
a lifeless continent. Of all this quiet
putrefaction, of a turtle with nowhere to go
and this animal out-of-the-ordinary sanity,
constant the shores, the tide, the ocean
(the sun will be worshipped), there shall be left only islands.

Poema sobre el paro

Tengo una ventana que no llega a dar a una esquina.
Torciéndome, veo la calle, perpendicular.
Pero esas posturas forzadas, y más con los años...

De joven, nostalgia de viajes. Y ahora,
querer nada más que volver, y no puedo.
                                        Perdonen.
Ya sé que no hablo más que de mí.

Out of Work Poem

I have a window that doesn't quite give onto the corner.
If I crane my neck I can see the street, perpendicular to me.
But stretching and straining like that, what's more, at my age…

As a boy I hankered for travel. Now
I want only to go back and can't.
                                    Please forgive me.
I know I am always going on about myself.

NINFA

De lo que no tenéis.
Hecha de lo que no tenéis, decretada imposible.
De que el árbol retoña y vosotros y yo no sabemos.
De lo que no será y lo que se teme.
Hecha de lo que debo huir. Sola. Invisible,
no ya de la ciudad, de cada uno,
no me ayudará el monte, no me devolverá la muerte, y sigo.
Si un momento olvidada en la retama
me hacen querer ser árbol, Dafne, o algo,
Casandra, hermana mía, como la destrucción,
sé que debo seguir. Que este dolor que tengo es mi venganza
inevitablemente, dada como las flores
por lo que no tenemos: lo poco que ellos lloran
por mis mares de llanto.
Mi llanto por lo que no puede dejar de ser.

NYMPH

I am made of what you do not have.
Of what you do not have, decreed impossibility.
Of the fact that the tree is in leaf again, not you and me.
Of what will not be and is feared.
Made of what I must shun. I am on my own. Invisible,
not just to the city now, but to everyone. There is no
recourse in the hills, death will not give me up; I go on.
If for one moment forgotten, in the broom,
they make me want to be a tree, Daphne, or something,
Cassandra, my sister, like destruction,
I know I must go on. That sorrow is my revenge,
inevitably, given like flowers,
for what we do not have: what little they cry
for my seas of tears.
My tears for what cannot fail to be.

Puntos de vista sobre las sirenas

I

Eres esa resbaladiza faz, te burlas
y con el agua y con tus compañeras
te has anulado a ti en tu grupo en mar
y en roca tu sustento para verte viscosa
total olvido tanto y doloroso
por no ser una o por ser muchas caras
mar roca y sacudidas rítmicas inclinándote.

II

Clama la playa por la tempestad. Elevas los ojos, sirena.
No miras la raya del mar en la playa.
Carente de tiempo destilas sabor de ti misma y te mojas.
La gente del tiempo entretanto reclama milagros.
¡Ay, que ni tú seas desesperada
y te veas sirena como te nombro yo!

III

Quien acompasa al mar su movimiento
no podrá distinguir si gime o canta
y eso es una sirena. Silenciosa,
profiere una continua voz, resaca, luto: un acompañamiento para algo.
Sollozar en el vendaval o, voceando,
llorar salpicaduras: se distingue
sólo la gota del abismo, nunca
distinguirá el agua del agua nadie.
De la continuidad de su sonido,
del impecable gozo o sufrimiento,
del animal dolor de perro, colmo
de simetrías, llueve

Points of View on Mermaids

I

You are that ungraspable, mocking face
intermingled with those of your own kind,
in sea, on rocks, on which you were propped,
only to learn you are a viscous substance,
obliviated, so great and painful is it
not to be a single face or to be several,
sea, rock and rhythmically shaking sway.

II

The beach clamors in the storm. Mermaid, your eyes.
do not lift to where the sea meets shore. In haste
you dive, releasing your own particular savor.
Mortals, meanwhile, ask for a miracle.
Oh, may not even you grow desperate
and see yourself a mermaid, as I declare you!

III

Anyone whose life is attuned to the sea
will be unable to say if it sings or moans,
and that is a mermaid. Silently intoning
a continuous voice: an undertow, mourning,
accompaniment for something.
A sobbing in the gale or a voice calling
in splotchy tears; but we
can only tell a drop of water from the abyss,
unable ever to tell water from water.
From out of pouring sound it rains –
the impeccable delight or misery
of a dog-like pain, the culmination

de abajo a arriba y vienen olas, llantos,
diferencias difíciles. Canciones, dicen algunos. Dicen,
ungidos ellos de la arena de la playa,
que han oído cantar y les da miedo.

of symmetries. It is raining
from down to up, and waves wail
difficult differences. They are songs, men say,
who are anointed with grit from the shore,
who have heard the singing and are afraid.

Ermitaño

Reticente a los edificios huiste
y abrigaste con lentas plantas tu soledad.
Años de condiciones: decías, cuando pueda ver,
decías, si tengo mi ámbito…
Ha pasado una vez una mujer. Han sido
años lentos de espera. Tal vez seas un viejo
y un ermitaño, como piensan, porque
una espera muy larga es devoción.
No supiste, no viste. De repente
sabes mirar la bruma del sol de la mañana
y el campo de verdad, explicaciones
de una espera vuelta hacia atrás.

De cada hoja, de repente hermosa,
cuelga hace tiempo desesperación.

Hermit

Mistrustful of what men built, you fled,
your solitude protected by the slow life of plants.
For years you set conditions: when I can see,
you said, when I come into my own…
A woman went by once. You waited
a long time. Maybe you are an old man
and a hermit the way they think because
waiting for a long time is a kind of devotion.
Not realizing, not seeing. Suddenly
you know how to look at the morning sun's haze
and the true countryside, explanations
for a wait unfolding behind you.

From every leaf, suddenly beautiful,
desperation has been hanging for some time now.

Casandra

Vosotros habláis desde el campo. Yo hablo
donde el viento ha derribado la catedral
y mientras yo viva es intrusa la hierba.
Decís que lo olvide, que la piedra es piedra y los otros
estaban conmigo tan sólo porque era pequeña
(«Casandra, te han hecho Casandra
las tropas y la tempestad»). Vuestros robles,
mis ruinas, mis costumbres son por igual recuerdos
de aquel horror. Cobardes. Los soldados
no hubieran hecho falta. Aquí se queda
la ciudad, que soy yo, mientras yo viva.

Cassandra

Friends, you speak from the country; I speak
from where the wind has knocked the cathedral down,
and so long as I live grass is intrusive.
You say, let it go, stone is stone, the others
went along with you because you were young
("Cassandra, the soldiers, the storm
have made you Cassandra"). Your oak trees,
my debris, my customs, are memories
of that horror. Cowards. The soldiers
would not have been necessary. Here is where
the city remains, and it is I, so long as I live.

Pastor llega, descubre el mar

Puedes volver atrás, dejando aquí una huella de cenizas.
Puedes pero —¿cómo decirlo sin rubor?— nada será lo mismo.
Esto es como una muerte: desde ahora,
vivir en una orilla, en una patria, en una
rebanada de tierra.
Puedes echarte a andar, de lado a donde seas extranjero,
mentir allí, decir que has naufragado,
hecha tu casa inalcanzable y cálida
por una tempestad que a pesar tuyo
nunca existió.
Puedes quedarte aquí, pasar a ser un loco.
Pedir que no le pase a nadie más, que aprendan
que aquí hay un mar, viéndote tiritando.
Puedes quedarte aquí, boquiabierto en la lluvia.
Boquiabierto en la lluvia, puedes quedarte aquí.

A Shepherd Arrives, Discovers the Sea

You can go back, leaving a ring of cinders.
You can but – how say this without blushing? – nothing will be the same.
This is a kind of death: starting from now,
living on a shore, in a country, on a
slice of earth.
You can start walking, over where you're foreign,
tell lies there, say you've been shipwrecked,
your house made snug and unapproachable
against a storm that despite you
never existed.
You can stay here, come to be a crazy man.
Ask that it not happen to anybody else, that they learn,
that here there is a sea, as they watch you shiver.
You can stay here, mouth open in the rain.
Mouth open in the rain, you can stay here.

Rambla

Lo que hay abajo es poco
más que lo que hay arriba. En esa dirección
dejamos sin embargo de aspirar a la huida.
Y no es el sol:
es el lugar del sol.
Y no es el mar, es la humedad del mar.
Y no es el cielo, es un estanque de aves.
Y no, para el viajero verdadero
una luz amarilla resume una ciudad.
Y eso es saber amar: no el mar, sino eso
que no es el mar al eje de un viaje de regreso.

Rambla

What lies below is little
more than what lies ahead. In that direction,
though, we stopped trying to escape.
And it's not the sun:
it's the place of the sun.
And it's not the sea, it's the damp of the sea.
And it's not the sky; it's a pond with birds.
And no, for the true traveller,
a yellow light can sum up a city.
And that's what it means to love; not the sea but
what the sea is not, at the hub of a voyage back.

de *De lo que viene como si fuera* (1990)

U̲p̲s̲t̲a̲t̲e̲

Voy a aprender, ya viejo,
desastre de los iroqueses,
el después de la indignidad:
un habla postalcohólica
para mención de muertes, no derrotas,
no batallas, no pérdidas,
propia de fuente efímera
que en lugar desecado
nombra constelaciones
de un cielo frío, duro, y anterior a la escuela
y sostenido por los iroqueses.

from *About what is coming as if it were going* (1990)

Upstate

Now that I'm old I'm going to learn
disaster from the Iroquois;
a follow-up of indignity;
post-alcoholic speech
for the mention of deaths, not
defeats, or battles, or losses,
what you'd expect of an unlasting source
that in a dried-out place
names the constellations
in a cold, hard sky that predates school
and is sustained by the Iroquois.

La mala hierba

Quién fuera joven para, como
los verdaderos viejos, irse,
comer la mala hierba, tener unos brazos leñosos
como la mala hierba y que ellos llamen
a eso saber; dejar atrás, girando,
nada que no te deje (tiempos
ávidos de minutos), no por hojas del olmo o piedras,
sino la mala hierba, codos
para servir de horca, nudos, lazos
para el forastero y para ti,
vegetal árido provisto de un grito
y sólo vivo, o muerto, eximido de lágrimas.

The Tough Old Weed

Oh to be young, that I might
like the truly old, be off
to eat the tough old weeds, grow
sinewy arms like weeds and have that
be called wisdom; to leave behind, in a whirl,
nothing that does not quit you (times
greedy for minutes), neither for elm leaves or stones,
but a tough old weed, the bad sort,
elbows to serve as gibbet, noose and fetter
for the stranger and for you:
a juiceless vegetable tricked out with a scream,
barely alive, or dead, yet exempt from all tears.

Retrato

(Con JVF y con RSF)

Solo y sin sol, sin sexo y sin sintaxis,
rebatido por vientos hoy anécdotas,
naturaleza es hoy que le tiemble la mano,
hoja que cae con árbol y no sirve de hoja.
Le queda querer ver. Le haría falta
un autofoco, aparte de otras prótesis.
Imágenes de lo que debe ser y, por afuera,
cuando lo arreglen y lo dejen fijo
podrán jugar con él los niños, algo
mejor que ser voluta, casi tanto
(los juguetes se van perdiendo en las mudanzas)
como el vilano que un viento insensible
lanza hasta que se pierde en línea recta.

PORTRAIT

(With JVF and with RSF)

Alone and sunless, without sex or syntax,
refuted by winds now just a story,
he sees nature today in his trembling hand,
a useless leaf falling from a tree.
And still he wants to see. He would need a spotlight
shone on him and other sorts of prosthesis.
Images of what ought to be and, outwardly,
when they fix him up and have him just so,
children will find a toy in him, which is
better than being an ornament, almost
(toys get lost every time you move house)
like a bit of thistledown the wind so unfeelingly
blows along down the road.

Quebrado

Para sentarse, un desvencijamiento,
un almacén de polvo,
de lo que es algo si está en otra parte.
Para sentarse un esqueleto, un ángulo.
Y aunque hay que caminar, carne vestida,
sorteando automóviles y encuentros,
entre una hondura y otra hondura pálida
lo duradero son unas junturas
flexionadas, ni rectas ni tendidas,
al escribir. Corazón de los ruidos,
que yo no pinto nada.
Que en nombre de los muertos
que se usa siempre en vano,
esa postura es muda, no es mía y te combate.

Fractioned

For a place to sit, something ramshackle,
a storage-bin of dust,
of what is something if somewhere else.
A place for a skeleton to sit, a nook.
And even though one must walk, flesh
in clothing, dodging automobiles, the odd encounter,
between one pallid canyon and another,
what endures are the flexed points of union,
neither straight nor stretching,
when you write. Heart at the heart of noise,
I do not belong here.
And in the name of the dead,
whose name is always taken in vain,
that position is mute, not mine, and gives you battle.

Alacrán

Ya no envidio al eunuco, al enteramente aceptable,
ya no tengo nada que ganar del mar.
Para corro de fuego, me basta la piedra caliente
donde digo que vivo y se dice que estoy ocultándome
hasta que un mediodía decida al aguijón.

Scorpion

I no longer envy the eunuch, the one entirely acceptable,
and I have nothing to gain from the sea.
For a ring of fire, hot stone will do, where
I say I live and they say I am hiding
until one midday decides I shall sting.

Del movimiento del camaleón

Sé que mi coraza es fingida.
Muevo con dignidad,
yo, un intento de aplomo,
que veo demasiado,
por entre lo que veo
un saber de que duro lo que dura mi imagen.

On the Movement of the Chameleon

I know my armor is make-believe.
I move with dignity, I
do, an effort at aplomb,
I who see very well,
among the things I can see, know
I last as long as does my image.

Erizo

Por unos ojillos vivos
pago dieciséis mil púas.
No puedo esconderme, sino
fingir que no tengo ojos.
Muero si no engaño; a cambio
no sirvo para pelota.

Hedgehog

Sixteen thousand bristles pay I
for these lively little eyes. I have
no way to hide but to
pretend I have no eyes.
I die if not deceiving; but there is this:
I will not do as a handball.

Legado

El corazón déjaselo a los lémures,
marsupiales, medusas. Lo que dejes
déjalo a algo retráctil, no parásito, a un hijo
tuyo y del sobresalto y un tanto en extinción,
en entresijos de los cenizales
donde los suyos topen con tus restos.

Legacy

As for your heart, leave it
to the lemurs, marsupials, jellyfish. Whatever,
leave it to something retractile, un-parasitical, off-
spring of yours and alarm's, verging on extinction,
leave it in the intricacies of ashpits
where their kind will stumble on what's left of you.

Afilador

(Con A.G.)

¿Qué cuchillos le puedo bajar y a quién, en la calle vacía,
llama el afilador? Había dejado de pasar y ha vuelto
con el paro, el pasado y, técnicamente, la desesperación
y se le oye los sábados, en los interludios del estrépito,
cuando están más vacías las calles y, estando vacías,
se entienden un poco mejor.

KNIFEGRINDER

(With AG)

What knives do I take down to him and who
in the empty street does the knifegrinder call to? He was gone; now
he's back, with the past, with men out of work and, technically, desperation.
Saturdays you hear him, in the gaps punctuating the hubbub,
when the streets are less busy and, being less busy,
are a little better understood.

Gato muerto

Alguna forma clásica de inmerecida
supervivencia, ha vuelto,
¡oh gran lugar!, a contemplar tus patios,
tus descampados, tu cacharrería.
Va cayendo hacia arriba como se cae el tiempo,
blanco y negro, durante días, esperando a las ratas
perfectamente nítido, sin que las ratas lleguen
(no llega el sol).
Alrededor el polvo, las máquinas domésticas,
unos cascotes, unos ruidos sin voz.
Fantasma: presumido. Animal en la forma,
no va, tierra, a la tierra, sino que se va en humo
como el tabaco y como
las civilizaciones, con perdón. Se ha quemado
despacio, imperceptiblemente. Se notaba
sólo al tocarlo, en el dolor.

Dead Tom Cat

Like some classic form
of unmerited survival, he has returned–
oh august spot!– to contemplate your back yards,
your vacant lots, your pots and pans.
He's falling upwards the way time does,
black and white, days on end, waiting for the rats,
so plain to see, without the rats ever making it that far
(the sun does not make it that far).
Around him dust and household appliances,
a bit of rubble, voiceless noise.
He's a phantom: all his airs. Animal in shape,
he does not, like the earth, return to earth but rather
goes up in smoke like cigarettes and
civilizations (no offense). He has been burning
slowly, imperceptibly. You could tell that
only if you touched him, from the pain.

Letanía del Día de Difuntos

Hirió Bueso al Huerco
en el calcañare.
Hirió el Huerco a Bueso
en la voluntade.

I

La muerte en una ciudad circular
planearía arriba, como en tiempos, pero ésta
es un hombre en la esquina de ojos mansos que canta
con los que cantan al dejar los bares.
Siempre es más joven que el que no está muerto.

II

La luz de noviembre no llega al espejo.
Anticuados, la vida, el mobiliario
quieren saber qué hacen aquí.
La muerte no tiene pasado y los ha rebasado
como el alfil, en diagonal.
Nuestro saber acaba en que pensamos
que él es mejor que nada.

III

Ningún mausoleo, ningún ademán de recuerdo. Da su abolición
sujeta a criterios secretos. Tal vez lo propicien las fiestas:
celebran como él el momento, repiten,
no vienen tampoco de ninguna parte.

Litany for the Day of the Dead

> *Bueso wounded the Orcus*
> *in the heel.*
> *The Orcus wounded Bueso*
> *in the will.*

I

In a circular city death
would hover overhead, like in the old days, but in this version
he is a man on the street corner with unassuming eyes,
singing along with those who sing as they leave the bars.
He is always younger than the one who is still alive.

II

In November light does not reach as far as the mirror.
Furnishings, life, want to know what they are doing here,
they have seen better days.
Death has no past: it's gone over their heads
on the diagonal, like a chessboard bishop.
Our erudition ends in our thinking
that he is better than nothing.

III

No mausoleums, not a gesture of remembrance. He grants
abolition with secret criteria. Holidays are of some help:
honoring the moment, like him, they repeat,
they too come from out of nowhere.

IV

Danos un patio por lo menos, dicen
desprotegidos los que piden dios, un marco de cielo.
Lo que hay de dios es la destrucción de su vida.

V

De ninguna parte y no sabe cantar.
Vivir es en él ese estar apostado, venir
es en él haber muerto nosotros.

VI

Sólo es como nosotros cuando mata
pero la esquina es suya, los cuatro lados de la encrucijada.
Es de los nuestros, decimos, mira la sangre de otro.
Decimos: podemos pasar, somos muchos,
es de los nuestros, debe tener miedo.
Tenemos tiempo, él no.
Tenemos sangre, él no.
Y la pancarta: tú eres de los nuestros,
lo demuestras matándome;
tú eres alguien, yo quiero ser alguien muriendo.

VII

Por ser por fin de lo desconocido,
Por no ser: fiestas, tedios,
paredes de moluscos, lámparas amarillas.
Él, la corteza pura, cortando la corteza.

IV

Give us at least a patio, they say, feeling defenseless,
those who beg for a god, a framing sky.
What there is of god is the destruction of their life.

V

He's come from out of nowhere and he cannot carry a tune.
Living, for him, is all about taking up a post; arrival
for him, is in our having succumbed.

VI

He's only like us when he kills.
But the street corner is his, every side of the intersection.
He's one of our own, we say, just look at the other guy's blood.
We say: we can get by, there are a lot of us.
He's one of us, he must be scared.
We have time, he does not.
We have blood, he does not.
And the flag that is flying: you are one of our own,
you prove it by killing me;
you are somebody; I want to be somebody, dying.

VII

Because you are, after all, what is unfathomed,
because you are not: holidays, tedium,
walls with the slime of snails, lamp's yellow light.
And he is: pure crust, cutting through the crust.

VIII

Nada es mejor que nada.
Único ser pacifico, única soledad.
Única nada toda finalmente lograda.
Y así todos los días.

VIII

Nothing is better than nothing.
A single solitude, the only peaceful being.
The only nothing that has been achieved.
And so on, every day.

La muerte que mendiga para comprar droga

Un álamo de invierno, o en un rincón de la habitación
y no dice nada. O extiende la mano en la calle y parece
que lleva algo negro, parece demasiado joven.
La muerte que has dado, la muerte que así te ha pedido
son pasos, las muertes que cuentas minúsculas
en tu camino hacia un rincón, el recorrido blanco de papel
hacia un haz de uñas blancas en álamo
que no dice nada
ni ruega ni recoge ni es árbol ni eres tú.

Death Begging Money for a Fix

An aspen in winter or in a corner of a room
and it says nothing. Or it holds its hand out in the street and
it looks like it's got something black on, it looks too young.
The death you've given, the death that thus you were requested,
they are steps, the deaths you count infinitesimally,
on your way to a corner, on the blank paper journey
to a sheaf of white fingernails shaped like an aspen
that's not saying anything
and doesn't beg or receive or is a tree or is you.

Revenant

Una conspiración de golondrinas
silenciada de pronto en el crepúsculo.
Se ha perdido la tarde.

Tardes que vas perdiendo. En la quietud llegada como a traición,
                                                           [el álgebra
se ha ido del horizonte de entre cuatro paredes.
Una vez, o a la vez, se te ha muerto el espejo.

Muerto el espejo que educadamente
hacía de ti un fauno,
en interior sostienes una bombilla eléctrica.
Luces que vas perdiendo, sólo pides el sol
pero quieres decir: sol y un espejo.

Dejadme volar, orillas del mar, tardes
yéndose, voy pidiendo
un espejo absoluto transparente en el aire.
Yo prometo que vuelvo, uno de tantos, no me
vais a reconocer pero yo vuelvo,
orillas del mar,
tardes, cumplido algún pasado,
simplemente pasando, queriendo no dar miedo.
Mar, déjame pasar
–iba diciendo.
                    Pasa pidiendo como los mendigos.

Revenant

A conspiracy of swallows
gone silent suddenly at dusk.
The evening has been lost.

Your evenings lost. In the quiet, like a blow of betrayal, algebra
vanishes from the four walls' horizon. Once, all
at once, a mirror has gone out.

And with the mirror gone out
that so politely made you look like a faun,
you hold a lightbulb up inside. Lights
you are losing, all you ask for is the sun;
what you mean is: the sun and a mirror.

Let me fly from here, *sea, I beseech you,*
evenings receding, I long for
an absolutely transparent mirror in the air.
I promise to come back, one of many, you
won't know me but I'll be back, *by the*
sea, evenings
with a past that is ending, or simply come to an end, not wishing
to alarm anyone. Sea, let me go by,
— I was saying.
                And he goes by, the way beggars do.

Primero de mayo

> *Hasta entonces Eco había tenido cuerpo, no sólo*
> *voz; y sin embargo, aunque habladora, no podía*
> *usar del habla de otro modo que ahora.*
>   Ovidio, *Metamorphosis*, III: 360-361

Inicia una indecisa encarnación. Si no hiciera frío
o calor, y además los pulmones
destrozados...
¿Cómo empezar más que con un recuerdo
tal vez de esta mañana
dispersándose
más
unas personas con unas banderas
dispersándose más donde ha llovido
como llueve aquí en primavera
desde los árboles?
                Como llueve aquí en primavera
                  lluvia de acompañar amores.
De cada día, no; del recuerdo, no;
de los álamos vengo, no: yo no sé si vengo.
Pero ¿cómo empezar de otra manera?
Acompasé a la lluvia mis sentidos.
Quise el sol para estar desnudo. Empiezo.
Empiezo una indecisa
invocación para que no haga frío.
                Lluvia de primavera
                  de acompañar amores.
He sido dispersado
una de tantas veces.

May 1st

> *Until then, Echo had had a body, not just a voice;*
> *and yet, even though she was talkative, she could*
> *not use the power of speech in any way but the present one.*
> Ovid, *Metamorphoses*, III, 360-361

An indecisive incarnation begins. If only
it were not hot or cold, or my lungs
not shot to pieces… How to begin
except with a memory, maybe,
of this morning's
dispersal
and some
people with flags
even more dispersed where it has rained,
the way it rains here in the spring,
pouring from the trees.
                     The way it rains in the spring,
                     when rain is the tune for love.
Not out of memory or the everyday.
"From the poplars I come", no, I don't know
if I do. But what other way to begin?
My senses all fell into step with the rain.
I wanted the sun so I could go nude. I begin.
I begin an uncertain invocation
for it not to be cold.
                     Rain in the spring,
                     rain for love.
And I have been dispersed
one of so many
times before.

Ahasuerus

No he venido a traer la paz ni a traer nada.
He venido —sí, fuera de horas de visita— sin querer molestar.
Un buen rato, en la habitación donde, cuando no hay visitas, hay polvo,
he escuchado unas espirales, con timidez.
He hablado, creo, y me arrepiento. Valgo
lo que el pretexto de mi origen, que me abrió la puerta.
Hay cada vez más muebles en las habitaciones.
Yo, como siempre olvido que voy de paso, no traigo nada.

Ahasuerus

I did not come to bring peace or to bring anything at all.
I came, to be sure, after hours, not wishing to disturb.
For some time now, when there are no visitors there is dust.
I have listened, shyly, to spiralling words
and I have spoken, I think, to my regret. I am worth
what the pretext of origins is worth; it gave me entry.
Rooms have more and more furniture these days.
I forget, as usual, I am only passing through, and bring nothing.

Breve ensayo sobre la poesía

Ella existe en mis intersticios
y yo en los intersticios de las cosas.
Si cuando está no hay nada más que ella
desde fuera debemos ser minúsculos.

Brief Essay on Poetry

It is there in my interstices
and I am in the interstices of things.
If when it is here there is nothing else,
we must seem so small from outside.

de *Religio y otros poemas* (2005)

RELIGIO

Seis misterios

Gratia gratum faciens
Tomás de Aquino

¿Quién es ésta que sube del desierto como varas de humo?
El libro de los cantares de Salomón, III, 6 (La Biblia del Oso)

from *Religio* and other poems (2005)

RELIGIO

Six Mysteries

Gratia gratum faciens
Thomas of Aquinas

Who is that coming up from the wilderness like columns of smoke?
The Song of Solomon, 3: 6 (La Biblia del Oso)

Primer misterio

Lu, sílaba simiente, motivo de la lengua,
hacia ti no se va: se vibra. Surges
y no hay aquí ni allí.

*

El aire te es lo que la arena al oro:
tu lugar natural.

*

Lu, mi panal, el punto del que parte
la rosa de los vientos,
te necesita el aire.
Eres el resultado de las flores,
no hay más volver que a ti.

*

Lu que bailas inmóvil, oro de aire,
sonrisa de la luna a mediodía,
haces aparecer el campo. Tengo
lugar.

*

Mi Lu, mi sol de calidad de luna,
única verdadera curva, llamo
tu movimiento al mundo trazado desde ti.

*

Mencionaba la luna, Lu, la luna.
La luna, que no sirve para nada
menos mover el mar.

FIRST MYSTERY

Lu, seed-syllable, setting the tongue in motion,
one does not move towards you, one vibrates. You arise,
and there is no here nor there.

                *

The air is to you as sand to gold:
where you naturally occur.

                *

My honeycomb, Lu, point of
departure of the compass-rose.
The air has need of you.
You are what comes of flowers,
no going back but to you.

                *

Lu who dances unmoving, like aerial gold,
the smile of the moon at midday,
you make the field appear. I take
place.

                *

My Lu, my sun in the guise of moon,
the only true curve, I call
your movement to the world
adumbrated by you.

                *

I mentioned the moon, Lu, the moon,
the moon that has no point but to
move the sea.

*

Lu, tiniebla que mira, claridad que se abate,
forma del pánico,
eclipse Lu, que muestra el universo.

*

Líquido vertical, aire posado:
eres el corazón del espejismo,
agua de pura luz.

*

Lu, columna en el aire, enteramente exenta.

*

Luz en la luz, mi Lu, morada comestible,
miel de aire, aire de miel,
se muerde en ti un romero que no se acaba nunca
y se es romero, desapercibida
hierba de olor.

*

Lu, a staring gloom, abashing clarity,
a kind of panic,
an eclipse, Lu, that shows up the universe.

*

Liquid plumb-line, settling air:
you are the heart of the mirage,
so much light you are water.

*

Lu, aerial column, wholly unencumbered.

*

Light inside of light, my Lu, edible abode,
aerial honey, honeyed air, your unending
rosemary in our mouth,
and one is rosemary, unapprehended,
a fragrant herb.

Segundo misterio

Oscuro cielo, pronto
ni cielo, todo
te ronda, Lu, turbulencia del tiempo.
Ya estás y no has llegado.

*

Tanto vivir y sólo era una espera.
Eres visible, Lu, como se oye el relámpago.
Lu, nombre de un lugar anterior a las aguas,
nombre de despedida, no nos dábamos cuenta
y éramos imposibles.

*

Qué viento tan fuerte nace de ti, Lu,
qué aparición eres, que nos expulsa.
Qué insignificancia no ser tú, de pronto.

*

Pilar de la tormenta, Lu, todo va arrasándose.
Eres la calma y la devastación.
Espesa luz que instaura un tiempo transparente,
eres el centro, Lu, se te puede cruzar.

*

No existe un desde arriba.
Latido Lu, misericordia muda,
el ansia era el descanso.

*

Second Mystery

Dark sky, soon
not even sky, all
surrounding you, Lu, the turbulence of time.
You are here already and have not arrived.

*

To have lived so long and it was for this.
You are visible, Lu, the way one hears lightning.
Lu, naming a place from before the waters,
a name for goodbyes, we did not realize it
and we were impossible.

*

How strong the wind arising from you, Lu,
what an apparition you are, you throw us back.
How insignificant not to be you, suddenly.

*

Pillar of the storm, Lu, all is being razed.
You are the calm and the devastation.
A thick light instituting a time of transparency,
you are the center, Lu, you can be traversed.

*

There is no from-on-high.
A pulse, Lu, a dumb-mouthed mercy.
Anxiety an interlude.

*

Así el calor aplicado a la piedra.
Lu, cavidad del sueño que precede a la caza,
el requisito del amanecer.

*

Patria de pasmo y despertar que dura,
símbolo del silencio,
reinas como reinaba el tiempo pero
tú no resumes.

*

Lu, que me has dado la respiración,
Lu, surtidor de pájaros.

*

Hablas, repueblas. Qué pequeña eres
ahora que hay mundo porque tú has venido.

Just like warmth applied to stone.
Lu, the cavity of a dream that goes before the chase,
requirement of the dawn.

*

Country of awe, awakening that endures,
symbol of silence,
you reign the way time reigned but
you do not condense into memory.

*

Lu, who has given me breath,
Lu, a rising spray of birds.

*

You speak, you people anew. How small you are,
now there is a world because you have come.

Tercer misterio

Alguna vez sí estás ausente, Lu,
y entonces somos como el gato hambriento,
una presencia atroz ante sí mismo.
Pero tú das paciencia a las raíces,
reconoces la vida en el frío.
Hay un vacío y de repente cantas
imperceptiblemente.

*

Eres la fiebre de lo que florece.
Como el que trae regalos y piensa que son poca cosa,
como el que tiene hijos y sabe que nunca ha de hacer lo bastante,
tememos la esperanza.

*

Vienes de dentro, Lu, sólo nos falta verte.

*

Rumor de las ramas, olor del barro,
sosiego de la madrugada, eres
lo que hace ver.

*

Lu, perfume, alhucema, no hay nada sin rocío,
has desmentido a todos los metales.

*

Eres como un recuerdo que esperara,
una nostalgia enfrente. Siempre te hemos sabido.
Razón del horizonte, no hay espacio sin ti.

Third Mystery

Sometimes you are indeed absent, Lu,
and then we are like famished cats,
a self-appalling presence.
But you teach patience to the roots,
you recognize life in the cold.
There is a void and suddenly you sing,
inaudibly.

*

You are the fever of what blooms.
Like one who brings gifts and thinks they are so poor,
or who has children and knows he can never do enough,
we are afraid to hope.

*

You come from within, Lu, we have only to see you.

*

Rumor of branches, smell of mud,
early morning calm, you are
what makes one see.

*

Lu, perfume, lavender, there is nothing without dew,
you have given metals the lie.

*

You are like a memory that was waiting,
a nostalgia before us. We have always known of you.
Reason for the horizon, no space without you.

*

Lu, siempre frente a mí cuando regreso,
tono del borde del amanecer.
No te hace falta dar. Tú no das, eres.

*

Lu, color que se toca. Nueva, anónima, fuente.

*

Lu derramable, lenta, que rodeas,
la que detiene, la que va cubriendo
los dos lados del pecho, la madre del cristal.
Lu, mi mirada misma, mis dos ojos abiertos,
mi ver, mi ser: nado en un mar que miro.

*

No hay más que un todo y se hace de la nada.

*

Lu, whom I always have before me when I come back,
a shade on the edge of daybreak.
You've no need to give. You do not give. You are.

*

Lu, color that can be felt. New, anonymous, a source.

*

Lu to be spilt, slowly, who envelops,
who pauses, who covers
both sides of the heart, mother of crystal,
Lu, my very gaze, my open eyes,
my seeing, my being: I swim in a sea of contemplation.

*

There is but a whole and it is made of nothing.

Cuarto misterio

Están tiroteando a una gacela.
Lu de violencia frágil, Lu pequeña, insegura,
compasión pura. No hay dios compasivo
hasta el punto de la inseguridad.

*

Cuántas veces te apartan,
qué estruendo de cascotes para disimularte
en lo deliberadamente polvoriento.
Hay la aridez y está tu llanto, Lu,
tu testimonio.

*

Mayor que lo más grande
y apenas un atisbo.
Pájaro y vuelo.

*

El mal, mi bien, tú que no eres el bien
como el papel no es trazo.

*

Qué bien abres los ojos, con todo dentro, Lu.
Qué mirada admirada, como si todo fuera
más arriba y benévolo y una larga respuesta.
Cómo bendices con una pregunta silenciosa.

*

Fourth Mystery

They are gunning down a gazelle.
Lu fragile in violence, Lu small and insecure,
pure compassion. There is no god compassionate
unto insecurity.

*

How many times they keep you away,
such a thunder of rubble to disguise you
in the dust deliberately raised.
There is dryness and your tears, Lu,
your witness.

*

Greater than the greatest,
and scarcely a glimpse of you.
Bird and flight.

*

Evil, my love, my boon, you who are not a boon,
just as a piece of paper is not writing.

*

How well you open my eyes, with all within, Lu.
How astonished my gaze, as if everything
were further above and benevolent and long in reply.
How you bless with a silent question.

*

Eres opaca y transparente, pozo
de luz, condensación oscura
de un infinito
intacto.

      *

Vas fundando el espacio,
das sitio a los fragmentos.
Fluye de tu piedad la piedad de las cosas.

      *

Sales, Lu, como sale el sol, a acompañarnos.

      *

Aquí del todo y sin embargo todo
definitivo como los recuerdos.
Sólo tú creas lo que ya existía,
nos regalas su calma.

      *

Lu, caudal y camino de las cosas,
¿cómo es que me distingues?
Tanta verdad, Lu, y ya no soy obstáculo.

      *

Te canta el tiempo, Lu.
Lu, gratitud en flor, amor en rama,
te canta el tiempo.

You are opaque and transparent, a well
of light, a dark condensation
of an intact
infinite.

                *

You are slowly founding space,
you make room for the fragments.
The pity of things flows from your pity.

                *

You come out, Lu, like the sun, to keep us company.

                *

Altogether here and nevertheless
as definitive as memories.
Only you create what already existed,
you give us the gift of its calm.

                *

Lu, wealth and way of all things,
how is it you distinguish me?
So much truth, Lu, and I am no longer an obstacle.

                *

Time is singing to you, Lu.
Lu, gratitude in bloom, love on the laden bough,
time is singing to you.

Quinto misterio

Ruido de paz, Lu, vida del paisaje,
eres extensa como
la aceptación.

*

No se te alcanza con itinerarios.
Ni urgencia ni renuncia ni
memoria amarga.
Pones asombro y agua en el pasado.

*

Lu, tiritar del despertar del mundo,
tú eres la lluvia y ningún dios es lluvia,
ningún dios sube como tú, bajando.

*

No hay límite a la tierra cuando llueve.
Laguna Lu, silencio acompasado,
tu superficie es música.

*

Tu superficie, Lu, donde se encuentran
cuatro elementos.

*

Eres sed, Lu, la sed que ha averiguado el agua,
eres el horizonte dentro. Enfrente,
tú, vapor de verdad, emanación de todo.

*

Fifth Mystery

The noise of peace, Lu, life in our surroundings,
you are vast like
acceptance.

*

You are not reached by itineraries.
Neither urgency nor renunciation nor
bitter memory.
You pour water and amazement on the past.

*

Lu, the shiver of the world awakening,
you are the rain and no god is rain,
no god ascends like you, coming down.

*

There is no limit to the earth when it rains.
Lu a lagoon, silence keeping time.
On your surface, music.

*

Your surface, Lu, where four elements
meet.

*

You are thirst, Lu, the thirst that water learned of,
you are the horizon inside. You, in front of me,
cloud of truth, emanation of all things.

*

Lu, transcurres, remansas, rebosas y rezumas.
Acarreas, devuelves, anegas y recorres
y no te vas.

*

Eres un río que corriera en olas.
Lu, por ti todo es justo, todo es innecesario.
Eres como si no existieras, sabe
sólo de ti quien está ya rendido.

*

Beben de ti los árboles. Dan a ti las ventanas.
Más acá de los labios
todo llega contigo,
con el ver y el beber y el respirar de ti.

*

Lu resuena de Lu.
La voz es ella misma.

*

Las palabras son ondas
concéntricas de Lu.
Habla. Expande el espacio.
Háblame, Lu, con esos ojos, háblame.

Lu, you transpire, pool, spill over and ooze.
You haul, give back, overwhelm and overrun
and you do not go away.

*

You are a river of waves.
Lu, thanks to you, all is just, free of necessity.
You are as if you did not exist, only he
who has already surrendered knows you.

*

The trees drink of you. Windows give on to you.
On the hither side of our lips
everything comes with you,
with seeing and drinking and breathing you.

*

Lu echoing with Lu.
The voice is selfsame Lu.

*

Words are Lu's
concentric circles.
Speak. Make space expand.
Speak to me, Lu, with those eyes, speak to me.

Sexto misterio

Como una nieve antigua
vive en el campo nuevo
brota donde estuviste
delicadeza.

*

Humo de movimiento,
vuelo de ave a la espalda,
tu paso es unas notas
que el aire deposita en nuestros ojos.

*

Tus gestos ponen paz
entre final y origen,
arcos de acuerdo
que se ven apenas.

*

No vienes, te renuevas.
Otro día, otra Lu.
Das una confianza
como de árbol que crece.

*

Lu, te has anticipado a la esperanza.
Qué gratitud por el deseo, cuánto
reconocemos lo desconocido.

*

Sixth Mystery

The way an ancient snow
inheres in a new field,
where once you were,
delicacy puts forth a bud.

*

A smoke-signal of movement,
the flight of a bird at my back,
you pass and the air
drops music into our eyes.

*

Your gestures make peace
between origin and end,
arches of accord
all but unseen.

*

You do not accede, you who are always new.
It is another day, a different Lu.
You give self-assurance,
like a tree growing.

*

Lu, you did not wait for us to hope.
How grateful we are for the desire, how
we recognize the unknown.

*

Se ha detenido un rayo.
Su claridad se queda con nosotros.

*

Alma de la madera, vertical de las llamas,
espuma de las olas de las sierras,
parpadeo del yermo.
Lu, lo vivo en lo vivo, lo cálido en lo inerte.

*

Vivo de ti y en ti.
Se ha disuelto el afuera,
mundo sin ti como un abismo horizontal.
No hay acogerse a ti, sino dejarse.
A cambio, nada.

A flash of lightning pauses in mid-air,
its clarity still with us.

*

Lu, you are the living in the living, what is warm in the inert.
Soul of wood, plumb-line of fire,
foam of the waves of mountains,
a desert's blinking eye.

*

I live by you and in you.
What is outside has dissolved,
world without you, a horizontal abyss.
There is no approaching you, instead one lets go.
In exchange, nothing.

Espectro brevemente

> *Een schilderij die spreekt, een spook van weinig'uren.*
> Constantijn Huygens, *Een Comediant*

> *A una señora mayor que vivía sola e imaginaba visitas*
> *de vivos y muertos, que siempre la dejaban sin despedirse.*

Esa televisión tuya de espectros
a falta de presente
se enciende y se apaga sola, como el presente,
ciudad de puras desapariciones.
Hace familias de lo que no ha llegado, de las
intemperies pequeñas, las infidelidades
del electrodoméstico, lo que, en tiempos perdidos,
era querer abrazos y no saber de quién.
Vienen como a tomar el té, como si estar aquí fuera lo lógico,
como si hubiera tiempo y gana y gente
para colgar los cuadros. Y se van como vienen
(con la lógica antigua de llegar para nada
y una técnica nueva para dar soledad)
a sus ocupaciones, al vacío, insistente
promesa incumplida de amor.
Y así habremos sido y son ellos:
como las hojas en el torbellino.

* * *

La esperanza es interminable, intermitente,
funciona, como los televisores y la vida, mal.
Hemos vivido hasta acabar traidores
o morir, que es lo mismo:
marchar sin despedirse,
venir sin cuerpo y sin voluntad propia,
ser poca cosa y anunciar desgracias,
repetir lo que fuimos,

A Specter, Briefly

> *Een schilderij die spreekt, een spook van weinig'uren*
> (A painting that talks, a ghost of a few hours)
> Constantijn Huygens, *Een Comediant* (An Actor)

To an elderly lady who lived by herself and imagined she received visits
from the living and the dead, who always left her without saying goodbye.

That TV set of yours with ghosts
for lack of a present
goes off and on of its own accord, like the present,
a city of disappearances.
It makes families of what has not come to pass,
small inclemencies, the infidelities
of a household appliance, of what was
for time out of mind a longing for warmth,
not knowing who would supply it.
They come as if for tea, as if to be here were only reasonable,
as if there were time and desire and people
to hang the pictures. And they go the way they came
(with the old story of dropping by for no reason
and a new technology to make you feel alone),
they go about their business, into the void,
a promise of love, stubbornly unfulfilled.
And so we will have been and so are they
like leaves whirling in the wind.

* * *

Hope is interminable, intermittent;
it works, like TV sets and life, badly.
We've lived long enough to become traitors
or die, which is the same thing:
leaving without saying goodbye,
arriving without a body and without a will,
not amounting to much and auguring misfortune,
recapitulating what we were,

cobrar tragedia en nombre del amor.
Cruzamos la ventana, como el vencejo,
para acabar así. Todos somos el mismo y el viento
para las hojas en el remolino.

* * *

Hemos vivido para que no nos cojan vivos
y aun a ti, que quisieras asirte a nosotros,
te eludimos con una displicencia de muertos, ásperos,
irónicos sin gracia, cumpliendo desganadamente,
un trámite trágico en ti. Porque en ti, que nos tratas de muertos,
vivimos como hemos vivido, unas ráfagas,
de las ausencias a las concesiones,
sólo rebeldes en el gesto y esta
capacidad de huir.
Sólo se sabe que nos vamos yendo,
desabridos, secándonos,
como las hojas en el torbellino.

* * *

Una vida con curso de murciélago,
fingiendo hasta la imagen de las rachas del viento.
Unos caminos vistos
a sacudidas para la pantalla.
No la verdad: lo póstumo. Máquina de sinopsis.
Porque tu vida es esta coincidencia de muebles,
todos somos el mismo.
Todos somos lo mismo y este viento que somos
y estos papeles en el remolino.

reaping tragedy in the name of love.
We dart past the windows, like martins,
only to end up as such. We are all the same person and wind
for the leaves set awhirl.

* * *

We have lived so as not to be taken
alive and even you, who would like to cling to us,
we avoid with a deadman's indifference,
a harsh and unamusing irony, reluctantly
complying with the red tape of tragedy.
For in you who behave as if we were dead,
we live as we always have, like gusts of wind
blowing from absences to condescension,
rebels in gesture alone and the ability
to take to one's heels.
All we know for sure is we are going,
ill-temperedly, and withering
like leaves set awhirl.

* * *

A life with the trajectory of a bat,
even feigning the image of a gust of wind.
Roads seen as if on screen
jerkily in fits and starts.
Not the truth: the posthumous. A synopsis machine.
Because your life is this coincidence of furniture,
we are all the same person.
We are the same and we are this wind
and these papers set awhirl.

Vox Clamantis

> *Non est lex*
> *Et prophetae eius non inuenerunt*
> *Uisionem a Domino.*
>   *Lamentaciones de Jeremías* 2, 9

No compraremos nada en Jerusalén, no nos detendremos en los mercados.
Lo hemos de cruzar a fin de llegar a unas piedras
iguales que éstas, al otro lado de Jerusalén.
Nos perderemos en la multitud, no queriendo verla,
y, dispersos, cada uno, solo, temiendo dejar esa piedra
que puede ser o puede no ser, hará ensayos
de voz de profeta, barítono para lagartos.
La desnortada soledad, la propia arbitrariedad del camino:
¿quién puede decir, si está solo, que no es el Mesías?

Vox Clamantis

> *Non est lex.*
> *Et prophetae eius non invenerunt*
> *Uisionem a Domino.*
>   Lamentations of Jeremiah 2: 9

We will make no purchase in Jerusalem, stopping in markets.
We will cross town in order to gain a few rocks
like these, on the other side of the city. We will
be lost in the crowd, not caring to see it, and each
of us, scattered, alone, afraid to quit the rock
that might or might not be the rock, will conduct
rehearsals in the voice of the prophet, a baritone for lizards.
A wilderness without compass, the arbitrariness of the road:
who can say, if he is alone, he is not the Messiah?

Víctimae Paschali Laudes

> Una forma de la esperanza, pese a todo: *También alguna vez no se ve la luz clara de los cielos, y pasa un viento, y límpialos*
> Job 37, 21

He aquí el tiempo de la resurrección,
un tiempo de túnicas blancas, piedras volcadas,
de indiscutido sol, lagartijas, romero.
Hay un tiempo como un lugar, como el liquen en el granito,
como la abolición del tedio de la infancia,
como no disputado a las basuras, un tiempo ascendente
devuelto vertical al sol, hipótesis
de abejas. Allí los hallazgos previstos,
prendas de juego, las camisas de las culebras,
todo lo que sabemos del futuro. Hay un, así,
moverse inmóvil fuera de verdades.
Y hay una guillotina de luz, pero qué importa,
sólo pensándolo, que se va siendo cada
vez más delgados, como los recuerdos,
inmaculadamente abejas, puro
futuro fue lugar.

Victimae Paschali Laudes

> *And now men see not the bright*
> *light which is in the clouds, but*
> *the wind passeth and cleanseth them*
>   Job 37: 21

Behold: the time of resurrection,
a time of white tunics, upended stones,
incontestable sun, lizards, rosemary.
There is a time like a place, like lichen on granite,
the abolition of childhood tedium,
not relegated to trash, as it were, an ascendant time
become a plumb-line in the sun, the hypothesis
of bees. Over there, foreseeable discoveries,
pieces for gaming, sheaths of snakeskin,
what we know of the future. So there is
an unmoving motion aside from truths.
And there is a guillotine of light, but what matter,
merely thinking it, how it gets
thinner and thinner all the time like memories,
immaculately beehood, a pure,
formally future place.

Encuentro una rata muerta en un jardín japonés

Había una rata. Estas son unas islas de calma
sólo muy lentamente mudables y orillas de un río
con la serenidad del mar, pero que fluye.
Todo un país se viene
de acá y allá del río, donde
mudamos tamaño según que sigamos senderos por entre los árboles
o abramos al mundo unos ojos en cumbre de monte
y un asombro lento
olvide los ojos, las cumbres y los que, minúsculos, pasan.
El caudal. Se hace tarde, u otoño, con sosiego,
soltamos dimensiones, somos lo que se olvida.
Disciplina de río grande: ribera muda
y gratitud al eco de todas las ausencias.
Nada es nada. Menos la rata, muerta, despatarrada,
diámetro exacto de una isla y réplica:
hay sí y hay no. ¿Es lo mismo? Es una rata
diciendo el silencio del río.

I Come Across a Dead Rat in a Japanese Garden

In their midst, a rat. These are islands of calm,
altering only very slowly, alongside
a river as serene as the sea but flowing.
An entire country
comes from here and beyond the river, where we
alter in dimension depending on whether we take footpaths between
                                                                                          [the trees
or open eyes to the world on a pinnacle
and a slow amazement
forgets about eyes, pinnacles and those, who, minusculely, go by.
The river-lode. It is getting late, or becoming fall, peacefully,
we let go of dimensions, we are what is forgotten.
The discipline of a great river: a soundless bank
and gratitude in the echo of all absences.
Nothing is anything. Except for the rat, dead and sprawling,
the exact diameter of an island and a reply:
there is and there is not. Is it the same thing? It is a rat
saying the silence of the river.

De *Apartamentos de alquiler. Obra reunida* (2013)

C.P. RESPONDE A CIERTAS OBJECIONES

Escurridizo, dices. Se escapa el agua, el aire.
Se escapa el fuego. Sólo
parece que la tierra
no se escapa. Parece.

From *Apartments for Rent. Collected Work* (2013)

C.P. Replies to Certain Objections

Hard to grasp, you say. Water
seeps out, so does air.
Fire seeps out. Only earth
is not seeping out, it would seem.

EL TIEMPO perdido,
el gris de la lluvia de marzo:
vueltas
en que no vuelve nada.

Time lost,
the gray rain of March:
a turning and turning
in which nothing returns.

Pueden caer historias porque hay lluvias constantes.
Es suave y triste lo que no ha pasado
y, es verdad, llueve como el
amor imaginado: en todas partes
verbos sin nombre sobre los tejados.

In the constant rain stories
can befall us. What did not come to be
is sad and smooth-edged,
and it's true, it rains
like the love we had imagined: everywhere
verbs without name on the rooftops.

El mar, que sólo sabe a sal, y el aire,
que sabe a sal, y el resonarse largo
de los mundos y el mar, hueco de bóvedas,
y el último segmento de la luna.

Y en gratitud que mido
rabitos de palabras.

THE SEA, that only smacks of salt, the air's
smack of salt, and the long reverberation
of worlds and sea, a hollow of vaults
and the moon's final segment.

In gratitude I measure
the tail-ends of words.

A UNA AUSENTE

Había estado allí contigo. Veo
otras tardes también hermosas, lentas,
con montes a los lejos.
Hoy se veían claro, iluminados
por la luz alargada del invierno.

Monótona ternura, quisiera que esto fuera
nada más que otro día.

Cómo nos une la melancolía.

To Someone Who Is Not Here

I was there with you. I see
other evenings too, beautiful, slow,
with hills in the distance.
Today they stood out clearly, glowing
in the lengthening light of winter.

Repetitions of endearment: I would have
this be like any other day.

Oh how we are joined in melancholy.

Sentadito en su tejado

Vendrá un tiempo también en que la gata Nora
sea vieja y se canse y esté siempre dormida.
Si no me he muerto, entonces seguiré como ahora
calentando la leche mientras ella me mira
o hace sus oraciones, como yo en torno al cazo,
en el suelo de la cocina.

La Europa protestante tiene gatos señores
que crecen, y envejecen, y así sigue la vida.
Aquí siguen, con suerte, los cuartos interiores
que no tienen salida.

Sitting Up On His Roof

There will come a time, too, when Nora the cat
will be old and weary and always asleep.
If I haven't died, then I will go on as always
warming the milk while she looks at me
or says her prayers, me over the saucepan,
her sitting on the floor of the kitchen.

Protestant Europe has lordly cats
that get fat and grow old and so life proceeds.
Here, with any luck, the rooms will still
not give onto the street, with any way out.

Nana de Gaza

Qué guapa en la cuna, mi niña adorada,
para que la muerte cuando venga a verte
te encuentre acostada.

Cierra los ojitos, vida de mi vida,
para que la muerte cuando venga a verte,
te encuentre dormida.

Duérmete, mi rosa,
para que la muerte cuando venga a verte,
sea cariñosa.

Duérmete, ojos bellos,
si hay gatitos muertos por entre las ruinas
jugarás con ellos.

Duérmete, rubí,
y a ver si la muerte cuando venga a verte
se me lleva a mí.

Gaza Lullaby

My dear little child, astir in your crib,
may Death find you sound asleep,
when he comes to pay his visit.

Eyes closed, my sweet,
so that Death when he calls,
will find you sound asleep.

Sleep, little rose,
so that Death when he calls,
will want to hug you close.

Sleep soundly, child,
kittens lie dead amid the debris;
you may play with them a while.

And now to sleep, my precious gem,
for when Death pays his visit, maybe, just maybe,
he will take me instead.

Cuento de Navidad y tal

Dice «¿De dónde sois?, que el niño
para inscribirlo la nacionalidad tal y tal cosa»
(yo ahí me perdí) y le dicen (se señalan)
«Turquía, y Paraguay».

Yo hasta entonces tenía mucho frío
y la aprensión, la angustia anticipada:
despacho de abogados de extranjería,
la espera, la diversidad de dramas,
el miedo, aquella gente
que aún no había visto y ya sabía triste.
De repente, la calma. Turquía y Paraguay.
Y el niño que está en la cuna.

En la estación del metro, saxo tenor tocando
«Las hojas muertas», y bastante bien.
A la salida noto escarcha nueva.
Queda luz en el cielo y cabe mucha
tarde esta tarde para ser ciudad.
Quitando las palabras, es inefable todo.
Vamos, diría yo.

A Christmas Tale, That Sort of Thing

Question: "Where are you from? It's the baby,
so we can get him registered, he needs a nationality…" and the clerk
[went on
(I couldn't make out any more) and then they say (pointing):
"Turkey and Paraguay".

Up until then I had been very cold and
anxiously anticipating:
the immigration lawyers,
the waiting, the different tales of woe,
the fear, all those people
I hadn't even laid eyes on and knew already were sad.
Suddenly, calm. Turkey, and Paraguay.
And the baby in his basket.

In the subway station a tenor sax plays
'Autumn Leaves' and it's pretty good.
I notice new frost when I exit.
The sky is still light and there's still lots
of evening left this evening, for a city.
Except for words, it's all ineffable.
Or so it seems to me.

Notes

Till the Future Dares: The title is from the poem 'Adonais' by Percy Bysshe Shelley, an elegy for Keats: "till the Future dares/ Forget the Past, his fate and fame shall be/ An echo and a light unto eternity!"

Here, Too, There Were Simple Elements: The epigraph from Dante, can be translated as "you were not made to live like ignorant animals".

Nabí: A *nabi* is the Arabic word for prophet, according to the *Diccionario de la Real Academia Española*. The Biblical verse in the King James version reads: "So Jonah went out of the city, and sat on the east side of the city, and there made him a booth, and sat under it in the shadow, till he might see what would become of the city" (*Jonah* 4: 5).

On my Tommy Gun, Knife, and Doll: The epigraph in old French means "The battle is marvelous and heavy-going". I translated "ametralladora", a kind of machine-gun, as a tommy gun, which was a word current for the guns used by famous criminals like Al Capone.

Points of View on Mermaids: In the early Christian era the mermaid crossed with the figure of a siren, imagined by the early Greeks as half-bird, half-woman. The sirens' song lured sailors to their death, as Ulysses is warned in a famous episode of the *Odyssey* (Book 12).

Cassandra: Cassandra, daughter of Priam and Hecuba, prophesies the fall of Troy but she is not heeded. Agamemnon makes her his concubine when he returns from war; her gifts are all degraded.

Upstate: The title is a reference to the region of New York State above the City. Carlos lived in Ithaca, New York from 1980–1983 and taught at Cornell University, which lies in the heart of Iroquois territory. See the book *Apologies to the Iroquois* (1970) by the American essayist and critic Edmund Wilson.

The Tough Old Weed: The phrase "mala hierba" (lit. bad grass) is a colloquial expression for the socially undesirable.

FRACTIONED: The Spanish offers an ambiguous title, which could mean "a fraction" or "broken". I looked for a way to suggest "fracture".

KNIFEGRINDER: An old occupation. Household knives had to be sharpened every so often and this was done by a man who walked through the streets with a wheel on which to whet knives and razors. He had a characteristic tune, which he played on a mouth organ, to alert residents he was in the vicinity. Carlos published a poem based on this one, titled 'Blues local para Antonio Gamoneda' in a booklet *4 Poemas de Carlos Piera* inserted into the December 1989 issue of the magazine *Zurgai* [Bilbao].

DEAD TOM CAT: The dead cat lies in an inner courtyard between buildings which is not easily accessed by tenants, though visible for days on end.

LITANY FOR THE DAY OF THE DEAD: The epigraph is from an old medieval ballad titled 'La muerte ocultada' [Death concealed], on a theme known as the Dismal Hunt. The Orcus is a mythical creature from hell – or perhaps the personification of hell – against whom the hero Don Bueso tests his mettle.

REVENANT: The title (French and English) refers to one who returns like a ghost from the dead. Lines 12 and 17 echo a poem by Luis de Góngora with traditional roots, 'Let me cry, (by the) seashore' (*Dejadme llorar, orillas del mar*). The Spanish is understood as a plea.

MAY 1ST: Line 15 is from a traditional medieval song: "From the poplars I come, Mother,/ To see how the wind makes them shiver" (*De los álamos vengo, madre,/ de ver como los menea el aire.*) The explanation is understood to be a veiled way of talking about a lovers' tryst. In the background is the quickening force of spring.

AHASUERUS: Ahasuerus is the Wandering Jew, an anti-hero who is doomed to keep walking the earth in punishment for his refusal to let Christ, who was bearing the Cross, rest his head against the wall of his home. In *A Remembered Future. A Study in Literary Mythology* (Bloomington: Indiana UP, 1984) Harald Fisch reads the myth in a revisionist mood as an historical archetype of endurance in the knowledge of guilt, without the certainty of regeneration or mission. Piera remembers being impressed with Pär Lagerkvist's novel, *La muerte de Ahasuerus* (1963) (*Ahasuerus död*, 1960), whose hero he remembers as an anti-Christ.

Religio: The quotation in the epigraph from Aquinas refers to a kind of grace of sanctification, a gift from God that allows the recipient to perform acts such as prophecy, speaking in tongues, etc.

A Specter, Briefly: Line 18, "leaves set awhirl". The image of spinning and whirling or spiralling crops up more than once in Piera's poetry. A spinning motion could in theory entail creation, says Juan Eduardo Cirlot in his *Diccionario de símbolos* (Madrid: Siruela, 2008). Or the motion of decrease. But, one might add, it could also suggest the pointless movement of a spinning top, which will eventually stop. The leaves call to mind a book's leaves and the impermanence of writing.

Vox Clamantis: "A voice crying". The epigraph is from Jeremiah's *Lamentations*, 2:9, in the *Biblia del Oso*: "[there] is no law. Nor did their prophets see God".

Victimae Paschali Laudes: I restore (and correct) the epigraph from Job, from the *Biblia del Oso*, which was missing in Piera's *Collected Work*. 'In praise of the paschal victims' is a title that refers to the Easter sequence in the Roman Catholic missal, which is sung from Easter to the following Saturday inclusively. Lines 7-8: "the hypothesis of bees", referring to the way bees seek orientation. The poem appeared in the single issue of the Spanish journal titled *Número de víctimas*, No. 1 (1991), devoted to protest of the 1990–91 Gulf War, into which the former President José María Aznar had drawn Spain. Contributors included Eugenio Trías, Luis Antonio de Villena and Ana Rossetti, among others.

I Come Across a Dead Rat in a Japanese Garden: The river is the Charles River in Boston and the garden is located in a museum in Boston, perhaps the Museum of Fine Arts. Line 10: "river-lode": my coinage, after the sense of *motherlode*.

C.P. Replies to Certain Objections: The four elements were defined by Empedocles and adopted by Aristotle.

Sitting Up on His Roof: The title echoes an old children's ballad 'Don Gato was sitting up on his roof'. About to be wed, the cat falls to his death but is revived by the smell of sardines wafting up from the marketplace. See Israel J. Katz and Roger D. Tinnell, 'Federico García Lorca as folklorist: the Ibero-American romance of Don Gato', *Anuario musical* 54 (1999): 253-311.

Gaza Lullaby: This poem was first published in a blog by Palinuro, the pseudonym of Ramón Cotarelo, in response to the bombing of Gaza in 2008-2009. It appeared in the Spanish journal *Sin permiso* (January 2009).

A Christmas Tale, That Sort of Thing: Line 12 is from a Spanish Christmas carol. Line 14: "Les feuilles mortes" [Autumn leaves] is a well-known love song from 1945 by Jacques Prévert.

www.ingramcontent.com/pod-product-compliance
Lightning Source LLC
Chambersburg PA
CBHW031322160426
43196CB00007B/631